Leadership Principles That Foster Healthy Team Development:

Introduction

Welcome to the future of leadership. This isn't just another manual. This is a blueprint for visionaries who refuse to settle for mediocrity. In the words of Steve Jobs, **"The people who are crazy enough to think they can change the world are the ones who do."** This manual is your guide to becoming that kind of leader—a leader who inspires innovation, demands excellence, and creates products and experiences that leave a mark on the world.

Chapter 1
Visionary Leadership:

Let's Think Different

The core of visionary leadership is the ability to see what others can't.
It's about looking at a blank canvas and seeing a masterpiece. Leaders
must cultivate the skill of envisioning a future that doesn't yet exist and
then mobilize their teams to bring that vision to life.

Challenge the Status Quo

Never settle. Always push the boundaries of what's possible. The
greatest innovations come from questioning the norm and daring to be
different. Encourage your team to think differently, embrace risks, and
see failure not as an endpoint, but as a steppingstone to success.

Focus on the User Experience

Leadership isn't just about leading people—it's about understanding and enhancing the experiences of those you serve. Whether it's your customers, employees, or stakeholders, their experience should be at the forefront of every decision you make. Design with the user in mind, and you'll create products and services that not only meet expectations but exceed them.

Building High-Performance Teams

Hire A-Players

Your team is your most valuable asset. Surround yourself with people who are not only talented but are also passionate about what they do. A-players attract other A-players, and together they create a culture of excellence. Remember, the quality of your team will determine the quality of your product.

Foster Collaboration

Innovation doesn't happen in isolation. It's the product of diverse minds coming together to solve complex problems. Create an environment where collaboration is not just encouraged but expected. Break down silos, facilitate open communication, and ensure that every voice is heard.

7 Principles to Foster Collaboration in the Workplace:

Principle 1: Lead with Heart

Collaboration begins with the heart. When you approach your team with genuine care and empathy, you create an environment where people feel seen, heard, and valued. It's about building connections that go beyond the job title. When people know that you care about them as individuals, they'll be more open to working together, sharing ideas, and supporting one another.

Principle 2: Create a Safe Space

A truly collaborative workplace is one where everyone feels safe to express their thoughts and opinions. It's up to you to create an atmosphere where diversity of thought is not only accepted but celebrated. Encourage your team to speak up without fear of judgment or retribution. When people feel safe, they're more likely to bring their best selves to the table.

Principle 3: Celebrate Every Voice

Every person on your team has a unique perspective and something valuable to contribute. Make it a priority to ensure that all voices are heard, from the loudest to the quietest. Actively seek out the ideas of those who might be hesitant to share. When you make room for every voice, you unlock the full potential of your team.

Principle 4: Embrace the Power of Listening

Listening is one of the most powerful tools for fostering collaboration. It's not just about hearing words; it's about understanding the emotions and intentions behind them. Practice active listening, where you fully engage with the speaker and respond thoughtfully. When your team feels truly listened to, they'll be more willing to engage in open, honest collaboration.

Principle 5: Model Transparency

Collaboration thrives in an environment of trust, and trust is built on transparency. Be open with your team about goals, challenges, and decisions. Share the "why" behind your actions and invite others to do the same. When you lead with transparency, you create a culture where people feel empowered to collaborate openly and authentically.

Principle 6: Encourage Shared Goals

Nothing brings a team together like a common goal. Foster collaboration by setting shared objectives that everyone can rally around. Make sure each team member understands how their efforts contribute to the bigger picture. When people are working toward a collective purpose, they naturally come together to support one another.

Principle 7: Practice Gratitude

Gratitude is the glue that holds a collaborative team together. Regularly acknowledge and appreciate the contributions of your team members. Celebrate successes, both big and small, and recognize the effort that goes into collaboration. When people feel appreciated, they're more motivated to continue working together and supporting each other.

Collaboration isn't just about strategies and processes; it's about creating a culture where people feel connected, valued, and empowered. Lead with heart, listen deeply, and celebrate the unique contributions of every individual. When you do, you'll create a workplace where collaboration isn't just possible—it's inevitable.

Empower and Trust

Great leaders empower their teams to make decisions. Trust your people to do their jobs and give them the autonomy to explore new ideas. Micromanagement stifles creativity.

Instead, provide clear directions, set high standards, and then get out of the way.

Chapter 2:

Driving Innovation

Stay Hungry, Stay Foolish

Never be satisfied with the status quo. The best leaders are perpetually hungry for more—more innovation, more improvement, more impact. They are also willing to take bold risks, even if it means looking foolish to others. Encourage a culture of relentless curiosity and fearless experimentation.

Simplify, Simplify, Simplify

Complexity is the enemy of execution. Strive to make everything as simple as possible. Whether it's a product design, a process, or a strategy, simplicity should be the ultimate goal. Simplicity isn't just about aesthetics; it's about clarity and focus.

Iterate and Improve

Perfection is a journey, not a destination. The most successful products are the result of constant iteration and improvement. Encourage your team to embrace feedback, learn from mistakes, and always look for ways to refine and enhance what they've created.

Leading Through Change

Embrace Change

In a rapidly evolving world, change is the only constant. Great leaders not only adapt to change but drive it. They are proactive in identifying trends and disruptions and are not afraid to pivot when necessary. Cultivate a mindset of flexibility and resilience within your team.

Communicate a Compelling Vision

During times of change, people look to their leaders for direction and reassurance. Clearly articulate the vision and the "why" behind the change. When people understand the purpose, they are more likely to embrace the journey.

Be Decisive

Indecision is the enemy of progress. As a leader, you must be willing to make tough calls, even when the path forward is unclear. Gather the best information available, consult your team, and then act. Decisiveness inspires confidence and momentum.

This manual isn't just a guide; it's a call to action. As you step into your role as a leader, remember that your job is to inspire, innovate, and leave the world a little better than you found it. Think differently, push the boundaries, and above all, stay hungry and stay foolish.

Think Different: Cultivate a Culture of Innovation

In the 21st century, leadership isn't just about managing resources; it's about inspiring a culture of innovation. The first step in creating an environment where creativity thrives is to challenge conventional thinking. Encourage your team to think differently, to push the boundaries of what's possible. Innovation comes when you're not afraid to question the status quo. As a leader, you need to foster a culture where new ideas are welcomed, not stifled.

Remember, innovation is not a one-time event. It's a process that requires continuous nurturing. This means creating spaces—both physical and mental—where your team can experiment, fail, learn, and iterate. Make it clear that failure is not something to be feared but a necessary step toward groundbreaking success.

Simplify to Amplify

One of the most powerful ways to lead in the modern era is through simplicity. In an age of overwhelming information and complexity, your job as a leader is to strip away the unnecessary. Focus on the essence of what you want to achieve. This not only clarifies your vision but also amplifies the impact of your actions. When leading your team, distill the objectives to their core elements. This clarity helps everyone understand the mission and align their efforts toward a common goal. The simpler the message, the more powerful it becomes.

Empower your team by removing the clutter, allowing them to focus on what truly matters.

Empower Individuals, Build Teams

The strength of a 21st-century leader lies in their ability to empower individuals while building cohesive teams. Each member of your team brings unique strengths and perspectives. Your role is to harness these differences to create something greater than the sum of its parts. Encourage ownership and accountability. When individuals feel that their contributions matter, they're more invested in the outcome. But remember, while individual brilliance is valuable, magic happens when these individuals collaborate. Facilitate a culture of open communication, where ideas flow freely, and collaboration is second nature.

Relentless Focus on the User Experience

No matter the industry, the end goal should always be the same: create something that genuinely enhances the user experience. Leadership in the 21st century demands an obsession with the end user. Every decision, every product, every service should be designed with the user in mind.

Teach your team to adopt this mindset. Whether it's designing a product, developing a service, or creating a marketing strategy, the focus should always be on how it benefits the user. This relentless pursuit of excellence in the user experience will not only set you apart from the competition but will also inspire your team to strive for greatness.

Vision with Execution

Finally, it's not enough to have a great vision—you must also be able to execute it flawlessly. A leader's vision is only as powerful as their ability to turn it into reality. This requires meticulous planning, an eye for detail, and the discipline to follow through.

Set clear milestones and hold your team accountable. Provide the resources they need to succeed, but also instill a sense of urgency. Execution is where vision meets reality, and it's in this space that leaders truly prove their worth.

In leading your team to create innovative and productive outcomes in the 21st century, remember to think differently, simplify your approach, empower your people, focus on the user, and execute with precision. These principles will not only drive success but also set the stage for transformative leadership.

Chapter 3

Creating Effective 21st-Century Leadership Teams that Foster Innovation and Promote Unity

The Power of Unity: Driving Innovation Through Collaboration:

In the 21st century, the most successful teams are those who understand the power of unity. Innovation thrives in environments where individual feel connected, valued, and inspired to contribute their best. As a leader, your responsibility is to create a team culture where collaboration is not just encouraged—it's a fundamental principle.

Start by breaking down silos. Traditional hierarchies often stifle innovation by isolating departments and ideas. Instead, promote cross-functional collaboration. Encourage your team members to work together, share knowledge, and build on each other's strengths. When your team functions as a unified entity, innovation becomes a natural byproduct.

Hire the Best, Empower the Individual

Building an innovative and unified team starts with hiring the right people. Look for individuals who not only possess the necessary skills but also share the vision and values of your organization. Diversity of thought and experience is crucial. It brings different perspectives to the table, which can lead to groundbreaking ideas.

Once you've assembled a team of top talent, your next task is to empower them. Trust your people. Give them the autonomy to make decisions and the space to take risks. When individuals feel empowered, they're more likely to take ownership of their work, leading to a more engaged and cohesive team. Remember, a unified team is not one where everyone thinks alike, but one where diverse idea is brought together toward a common goal.

Communicate with Clarity and Purpose

Effective communication is the backbone of any successful team. As a leader, your role is to ensure that everyone is on the same page. This doesn't mean micromanaging but rather providing clear direction and purpose. Your team should understand not just what they're doing, but why they're doing it.

Foster an environment of open dialogue. Encourage your team to voice their ideas, concerns, and feedback. When communication flows freely, misunderstandings are minimized, and unity is strengthened. A team that communicates well can innovate effectively because every member understands their role in the bigger picture.

Create a Culture of Mutual Respect

Innovation flourishes in environments where there is mutual respect among team members. This means valuing each person's contributions, regardless of their role. It's about creating a safe space where people feel comfortable sharing their ideas without fear of criticism or ridicule.

As a leader, model the behavior you want to see. Show respect in every interaction, and it will ripple through your team. When respect is ingrained in your team culture, it fosters trust and unity, creating a fertile ground for innovative thinking.

Lead by Example, Inspire Through Vision

Finally, remember that leadership is as much about action as it is about vision. To build a team that is both innovative and united, you must lead by example. Your team looks to you for guidance, so embody the values and principles you want them to adopt. Be the first to embrace new ideas, to step out of your comfort zone, and to support your team members. Inspire them with a clear, compelling vision of the future.

When your team believes in the vision and sees you actively working toward it, they will be motivated to follow suit. In creating a 21st-century leadership team that drives innovation and promotes unity, focuses on collaboration, empowers individuals, communicates effectively, fosters mutual respect, and leads by example. These principles will not only help you build a strong, cohesive team but will also position your organization to achieve extraordinary outcomes.

Chapter 4

Leadership Teams that Adapt to Changes in Upper Management

Embrace Change as an Opportunity

In the dynamic landscape of the 21st century, change is inevitable, especially in upper management. As a leader, your role is to prepare your team to not just survive these changes but to thrive through them. The first step in developing an adaptable leadership team is to shift the mindset around change. Instead of viewing it as a disruption, see it as an opportunity for growth and innovation.

Teach your team to embrace change with enthusiasm. When new leadership comes in, it brings fresh perspectives and ideas. Encourage your team to be open-minded, welcome new strategies, and see the potential for positive transformation. The ability to adapt quickly and effectively is what separates a good team from a great one.

Foster a Culture of Resilience

Resilience is the cornerstone of any adaptable team. Building resilience starts with cultivating a culture where challenges are met with creativity and determination rather than fear. Equip your team with the tools they need to bounce back from setbacks and remain focused during periods of uncertainty.

Encourage your leaders to stay calm under pressure and to approach problems with a solution-oriented mindset. When upper management changes, the entire organization feels the ripple effects. Your team should be the steady force that keeps things on track. By fostering resilience, you ensure that your team can maintain its effectiveness, regardless of the shifts happening at the top.

Promote Transparency and Open Communication

In times of change, communication becomes more critical than ever. A leadership team that is kept in the dark will struggle to adapt. As a leader, prioritize transparency and open communication. Keep your team informed about the changes occurring in upper management and how those changes may impact them.

Encourage your team to ask questions, voice concerns, and share their thoughts. Open dialogue reduces uncertainty and builds trust. When your team feels informed and involved, they are better equipped to adapt to new leadership. It's not just about managing the transition but about actively engaging with it.

Maintain a Strong, Unified Vision One of the biggest challenges when upper management changes is maintaining continuity. New leaders often bring new visions, but your team's core mission should remain intact. Ensure that your leadership team is aligned with the organization's long-term goals, regardless of who is at the helm.

Reiterate the importance of the organization's vision and values. Even as new ideas and strategies are introduced, your team's commitment to the overarching mission should not waver. A strong, unified vision acts as a stabilizing force, helping your team stay focused and motivated through periods of transition.

Encourage Flexibility and Continuous Learning

Adaptable leadership teams are flexible and committed to continuous learning. In the face of change, the ability to pivot and adjust strategies is invaluable. Encourage your team to be flexible in their thinking and approach. This might mean redefining roles, adopting new methodologies, or integrating different technologies. Support your team's professional development. Provide opportunities for them to learn new skills and to stay current with industry trends. The more adaptable and knowledgeable your team is, the easier it will be for them to navigate changes in upper management. Continuous learning keeps your team agile and prepared for whatever comes next.

Lead with Empathy and Support

Finally, understand that change can be unsettling. Lead with empathy and support your team through the transition. Acknowledge the challenges they may face and offer your guidance to help them adapt. Be present, be approachable, and be a source of stability. Your team will look to you for reassurance during times of change. By leading with empathy, you build a sense of trust and loyalty that will strengthen your team's ability to adapt.

In developing leadership teams that can adapt to changes in upper management, focus on embracing change as an opportunity, fostering resilience, promoting transparency, maintaining a unified vision, encouraging flexibility, and leading with empathy. These principles will equip your team to not just endure changes at the top but to emerge stronger and more effective.

Chapter 5

The Importance of Leadership: Professionalism, Compassion, Equity, and Inclusion

In any leadership role, professionalism is the bedrock upon which trust and respect are built. It's about setting the standard and being the example, your team can look up to. Professionalism isn't just about how you present yourself; it's about how you carry yourself in every interaction, every decision, every challenge. Your team needs to see that you're committed to excellence, that you take your responsibilities seriously, and that you're consistent in your actions.

But let's be clear, professionalism doesn't mean being distant or cold. It's about maintaining integrity and accountability while also being approachable. Your team should know that they can rely on you, not just because you're their leader, but because you're someone who consistently shows up, does the work, and upholds the organization's values Professionalism is the glue that holds a team together, especially when times get tough.

Compassion: The Human Element in Leadership

Leadership isn't just about hitting targets and achieving goals—it's about people. Compassion is what brings the human element into leadership. It's about understanding that your team members are more than just employees; they're individuals with their struggles, dreams, and lives outside of work.

When you lead with compassion, you create an environment where people feel valued and supported. It's about taking the time to listen, to understand where someone is coming from, and to offer help when it's needed. Compassionate leadership fosters loyalty and dedication because people are more likely to go the extra mile when they know their leader genuinely cares about them.

Remember, compassion isn't a sign of weakness; it's a strength. It shows that you're secure enough in your leadership to be vulnerable, to connect with your team on a human level, and to lead with your heart as much as your head.

Equity: The Pillar of Fairness and Justice

In today's world, equity is non-negotiable. As a leader, it's your responsibility to ensure that everyone on your team has access to the same opportunities, resources, and support. Equity is about leveling the playing field, recognizing that not everyone starts from the same place, and taking intentional steps to address those disparities. This means being aware of unconscious biases, challenging systemic barriers, and actively working to create a more just and fairer environment. Equity isn't just a policy—it's a practice. It's about making decisions that are fair and just, even when it's not the easiest or most convenient option.

When you lead with equity, you're not just benefiting the individuals on your team—you're strengthening the entire organization.

A diverse and equitable team brings a wide range of perspectives and ideas, leading to better solutions and more innovative outcomes. Equity is what ensures that everyone has a seat at the table and that every voice is heard.

Creating a Culture Where Everyone Belongs

Inclusion is about more than just having diverse voices in the room; it's about creating a culture where everyone feels they belong. It's about actively seeking out and valuing different perspectives, experiences, and backgrounds. Inclusion means making sure that every team member feels seen, heard, and respected. As a leader, it's your job to cultivate an environment where diversity is not just tolerated but celebrated. This means creating spaces where people feel safe to express their authentic selves, where differences are embraced, and where collaboration thrives. Inclusion is about recognizing the unique contributions that each person brings to the table and ensuring that those contributions are valued. When you lead with inclusion, you're not just building a stronger team—you're creating a more vibrant, innovative, and successful organization. Inclusion drives engagement, fosters creativity, and ultimately leads to better results. Incorporating, professionalism, compassion, equity, and inclusion into your leadership approach isn't just the right thing to do—it's essential for creating a workplace that thrives. These values are the foundation of effective leadership in today's world, and they're what will set you and your team apart. Lead with them, and you'll build a team and a community where everyone can succeed.

Chapter 6

Trust is the Foundation of Leadership

Trust is the Foundation of Leadership

In leadership, trust is the bedrock upon which everything else is built. Without trust, there can be no real connection, no genuine collaboration, and certainly no effective leadership. One of the most critical components of trust is confidentiality. When people know that what they share with you will remain private, it creates a secure environment where honesty and transparency can flourish. As a leader, you are entrusted with sensitive information—from personal issues to strategic plans—and how you handle that information speaks volumes about your integrity. Confidentiality is not just a practice; it's a principle that must be upheld consistently. When your team knows they can rely on you to keep their confidence, it strengthens their trust in you, which is the foundation of any successful team.

Confidentiality Fosters Open Communication

Open communication is the lifeblood of any thriving organization. However, for communication to be truly open, it must be safe. When staff members feel confident that their concerns, ideas, or challenges will be kept confidential, they are more likely to speak up. This openness allows for the free flow of information, which is essential for problem-solving, innovation, and growth.

Confidentiality fosters an environment where people feel comfortable sharing their thoughts without fear of judgment or repercussions. It encourages a culture where issues are addressed head-on rather than being swept under the rug. As a leader, your commitment to confidentiality is a commitment to creating a culture of openness, where honest communication is valued and protected.

Respecting Privacy Builds Stronger Relationships

Leadership is about relationships, and relationships are built on respect. Respecting the privacy of others is a fundamental way to show that respect. When you honor the confidentiality of the information shared with you, you demonstrate that you value the individual and their trust in you.

This respect leads to stronger, more meaningful relationships. When your team members know that you respect their privacy, they feel valued as individuals, not just as employees. This builds loyalty, deepens trust, and creates a sense of belonging within the team. In turn, these strong relationships lead to better collaboration and a more cohesive, effective team.

Protecting Confidentiality Safeguards the Organization

Confidentiality isn't just about protecting personal information; it's also about protecting the organization. Sensitive information—whether it's about company strategies, financial data, or personnel issues—must be handled with the utmost care. A breach of confidentiality can have serious consequences, from damaging reputations to legal repercussions.

As a leader, it's your responsibility to ensure that confidential information is safeguarded. This means setting clear policies, educating your team on the importance of confidentiality, and leading by example. By protecting confidential information, you're not just safeguarding the organization; you're also maintaining the trust that is vital to its success

Integrity is Non-Negotiable

At the core of confidentiality is integrity. Integrity means doing the right thing, even when it's difficult. It means keeping your word, honoring your commitments, and maintaining the highest ethical standards. In leadership, your integrity is your most valuable asset, and confidentiality is a key part of that integrity.

When you consistently uphold confidentiality, you send a powerful message to your team—that you are a leader they can trust, a leader who values their privacy, and a leader who will do what's right. This integrity is non-negotiable, and it's what sets great leaders apart.

In conclusion, confidentiality is not just a matter of policy; it's a matter of principle. It's about building trust, fostering open communication, respecting privacy, safeguarding the organization, and upholding integrity. As a leader, your commitment to confidentiality is a commitment to creating a culture of trust and respect, where your team can thrive. When you protect confidentiality, you protect the very foundation of your leadership and the success of your organization.

Chapter 7

Workplace Policy: Workplace Free from Sexual Harassment

The purpose of this policy is to ensure that our workplace is free from sexual harassment and to provide a safe, respectful, and inclusive environment for all employees. This policy outlines the standards of conduct expected from all employees, the procedures for reporting incidents of sexual harassment, and the consequences for violations of this policy. The policy is in alignment with the principles and regulations enforced by the Office of Civil Rights (OCR).

Policy Statement

Our organization is committed to maintaining a workplace free from sexual harassment. Sexual harassment in any form—whether verbal, physical, or visual—will not be tolerated. This commitment applies to all employees, including full-time, part-time, temporary, and contract workers, as well as to any other individuals who interact with our organization, including clients, customers, vendors, and visitors. Sexual harassment is a form of discrimination prohibited by Title VII of the Civil Rights Act of 1964, and it is our policy to enforce this prohibition fully. Every employee has the right to work in an environment free from sexual harassment and to be treated with dignity and respect.

Definitions

Sexual harassment includes, but is not limited to, the following behaviors:

1. Unwelcome Sexual Advances: Any unwelcome sexual propositions or advances, whether verbal, non-verbal, or physical.

2. Requests for Sexual Favors: Any request for sexual favors, whether explicitly or implicitly tied to employment conditions or opportunities.

3. Sexually Explicit or Offensive Conduct: Any conduct that is sexually explicit or offensive, including jokes, innuendos, gestures, or comments that create an intimidating, hostile, or offensive work environment.

4. Retaliation: Any adverse action taken against an individual for reporting sexual harassment, participating in an investigation, or opposing discriminatory practices.

Reporting Procedures

Employees who believe they have been subjected to sexual harassment or who have witnessed harassment in the workplace are strongly encouraged to report the incident as soon as

possible. Reports can be made to the following individuals or offices:

- Immediate Supervisor: Employees may report incidents directly to their immediate supervisor unless the supervisor is the alleged harasser.

- Human Resources Department: Employees may also report incidents to the Human Resources Department, which is responsible for handling complaints with confidentiality and professionalism.

- Office of Civil Rights (OCR) or Equal Employment Opportunity (EEO) Officer: Employees may report incidents to the designated OCR or EEO officer within the organization if they feel uncomfortable reporting to their supervisor or HR.

Reports should include as much detail as possible, including the names of individuals involved, specific conduct observed, dates, times, and any witnesses. Anonymous reports will be accepted, but the ability to investigate may be limited by the lack of detail.

Investigation Process

Upon receiving a report of sexual harassment, the organization will promptly conduct a thorough and impartial investigation. The investigation will be conducted in a manner that respects the

confidentiality of all parties fully involved. All employees are expected to cooperate fully with the investigation.

The investigation may include, but is not limited to, the following steps:

1. Interviewing the Complainant: The individual who reported the harassment will be interviewed to gather detailed information.

2. Interviewing the Accused: The individual accused of harassment will be interviewed and allowed to respond to the allegations.

The complainant wing Witnesses: Any witnesses identified by the complainant or accused will be interviewed to gather additional information.

4. Reviewing Evidence: Any relevant documents, communications, or physical evidence will be reviewed.

Consequences for Violations

If the investigation concludes that a violation of this policy has occurred, the organization will take immediate and appropriate corrective action. Disciplinary actions may include, but are not limited to:

- Verbal or written warnings

- Mandatory training or counseling

- Suspension without pay

- Demotion or reassignment

- Termination of employment

n addition, the organization will take measures to prevent further arassment and to protect the complainant from retaliation.

Non-Retaliation Policy

Retaliation against an individual who reports sexual harassment or participates in an investigation is strictly prohibited. Any acts of etaliation will be met with disciplinary action, up to and including ermination of employment.

Training and Education

The organization is committed to providing regular training and ducation on sexual harassment prevention to all employees. This raining will cover the definitions of harassment, how to recognize it, nd the procedures for reporting it. Supervisors and managers will eceive additional training on how to handle complaints and maintain a arassment-free workplace.

Maintaining a workplace free from sexual harassment is a shared esponsibility. Every employee is expected to contribute to a respectful nd safe work environment. By adhering to this policy and reporting any ncidents of harassment, we can ensure that our workplace remains nclusive, respectful, and free from discrimination.

This policy should be reviewed regularly to ensure its effectiveness and compliance with all applicable laws and regulations.

Imagine you're holding a beautifully designed product in your hand—a product that's been crafted with care, precision, and attention to detail. Every curve, every function, and every material has been chosen with one purpose: to create something people love. Now, think of your leadership team as the designers of this product. And the product? Your people—the lifeblood of your organization.

Focus on Experience, Not Just the Numbers

Just like we didn't build the iPhone by focusing on features alone, you can't reduce attrition by focusing solely on metrics. Get into the minds of your people. Understand their experience at every touchpoint—from onboarding to daily interactions, to how they feel about their future within your company. Your job is to craft an experience so compelling that leaving isn't even an option.

Simplicity: Remove the Friction

Great design is about removing the unnecessary. Look for points of friction that make people's work lives harder than they need to be. Is there too much bureaucracy? Are people bogged down by processes that stifle creativity? Simplify. Make it easy for them to do their best work. People leave when it's easier to go somewhere else than to stay.

Empower Through Ownership

We didn't just give people tools; we gave them tools they could own and personalize. Your leaders need to foster a culture where every team member feels like they own a piece of the company's success. When people feel ownership, they're invested—they don't just work for you; they work with you.

Inspire Through Vision

People don't join a company; they join a mission. They want to be part of something bigger than themselves. Leadership teams must continuously communicate a compelling vision that resonates on a personal level. When your team is inspired, they'll inspire others. Attrition happens when people lose sight of why they're here in the first place.

Design for Longevity, Not Just the Launch

We always designed our products to last—to be part of people's lives long-term. Think of your people's strategy in the same way. What are you doing today to ensure that your people will want to stay with you tomorrow? Regularly update your approach based on feedback. Continuous improvement isn't just for products; it's for people too.

Lead with Empathy

The most powerful tool in your leadership toolbox isn't a process; it's empathy. Understand your people's needs, dreams, and challenges. Be there when it matters. Sometimes, just knowing that leadership genuinely cares can be the deciding factor in whether someone stays or goes.

Create a Culture of Innovation

People stay where they can grow. Foster an environment where creativity and innovation are not just encouraged but expected. Allow people to experiment, to fail, to learn. When people feel they can evolve with the company, attrition becomes a non-issue.

In essence, cutting down on attrition isn't about enforcing stricter policies or offering more perks. It's about designing an experience so compelling that your people wouldn't dream of leaving. Just like with a great product, when you get it right, everything else falls into place.

Chapter 8

Aligning Vision with Purpose

Key 1: Aligning Vision with Purpose:

True productivity begins when vision aligns with purpose. A leadership team must first have a clear understanding of the collective vision that drives the organization. But vision alone is not enough. It must be deeply rooted in a sense of purpose—a purpose that transcends the mundane and touches the divine. Encourage your leaders to seek out the "why" behind the vision. When they see their work as part of a higher calling, their productivity will not just increase; it will multiply. They will move from merely managing tasks to executing them with a sense of mission. Let every strategy, every goal, and every decision be filtered through this dual lens of vision and purpose. This alignment is where true power lies.

Key 2: Fostering a Spirit of Unity:

The second key to a productive leadership team is unity. A house divided cannot stand, and a team fragmented by discord cannot produce the results it is destined to achieve. As a leader, it is your role to cultivate an atmosphere where unity thrives. This goes beyond mere collaboration—it's about creating a culture where each member honors the unique gifts and perspectives of others. Encourage your leaders to build bridges, not walls, to communicate with transparency, and to resolve conflicts with wisdom and grace.

When your team operates in the power of agreement, there is no limit to what they can accomplish.

Remember, unity is not the absence of differences but the harmonization of diverse strengths toward a common goal.

Key 3: Empowering Through Transformational Leadership:

Finally, a productive leadership team is empowered to lead transformation ally. This means moving beyond traditional, transactional leadership to one that transforms hearts and minds. Equip your leaders to be visionaries, mentors, and motivators. Teach them to lead by example, to inspire others through their own commitment to excellence, and to elevate those around them. Transformational leadership isn't about control; it's about influence. It's about lifting others as you climb, creating an environment where every team member feels valued, heard, and empowered to contribute at their highest capacity. When your leaders are transformational, they will not only drive productivity but also ignite a passion in their teams that fuels sustained success.

These three keys—vision with purpose, unity, and transformational leadership—are the pillars upon which a productive leadership team is built. When these are in place, your team will not just perform; they will thrive, moving from strength to strength as they lead with divine purpose and power.

The Buck Stops with You: Leadership in Project Management

Listen up, folks! Let me tell you something - leadership in project management isn't just about assigning tasks and tracking progress. It's about inspiring, motivating, and empowering your team to deliver results. And let me tell you, it's not easy.

As a leader, you're the one who sets the tone, makes the tough decisions, and takes the heat when things go wrong. But you're also the one who gets to celebrate the wins, see the impact of your team's hard work, and know that you're making a difference.

So, here's the deal. If you want to be a great project leader, you need to focus on a few key things:

Motivation: What drives your team? What gets them out of bed in the morning? Figure it out and use it to your advantage.

Performance Management: Set clear expectations, provide feedback, and hold people accountable. But also know when to give someone a break.

Communication: Don't just talk - listen. And don't just listen - act. Team Building: Your team is your greatest asset. Invest in them, support them and trust them.

Innovation: Don't be afraid to try new things. And don't be afraid to fail.

Strategic Management: Keep your eye on the prize. What's the end goal How does this project fit into the bigger picture?

Clarence, this all sounds amazing, but how do I appropriate?" Well, here's the thing - leadership isn't a formula. It's an art. And like any art, i takes practice, patience, and persistence.

So, go out there and lead. Make mistakes. Learn from them. And keep pushing forward. Because in the end, the buck stops with you. Here's the continuation of the chapter:

Motivation: The Spark that Ignites the Flame

You can't motivate someone who doesn't want to be motivated. But you can create an environment that inspires and energizes. Recognize and reward outstanding performance, provide opportunities for growth and development, and lead by example. Show your team that you care about their success and well-being.

Performance Management: The Art of Feedback

Feedback is the breakfast of champions. But only if it's constructive, specific, and timely. Don't sugarcoat it, but don't brutalize either. Find the balance. And remember, feedback is a two-way street. Listen to your team's concerns and ideas.

Communication: The Lifeblood of Project Management

Communication is key. But it's not just about talking; it's about listening actively, asking questions, and clarifying expectations. Make sure your team knows what's expected of them and why. And don't assume - confirm.

Team Building: The Power of Unity

Your team is your greatest asset. Invest in them, support them, and trust them. Encourage collaboration, empower decision-making, and foster open communication. Celebrate successes and learn from failures together.

Innovation: The Spark that Ignites Innovation

Don't be afraid to try new things. Encourage experimentation, calculated risk-taking, and creativity. Provide resources and support for innovation, and lead by example.

Strategic Management: The Big Picture

Keep your eye on the prize. What's the end goal? How does this project fit into the bigger picture? Align your project with the organization's strategic objectives and ensure everyone understands the why.

Now, I know what you're thinking - "Clarence, this all sounds great, but how do I put it into practice?" Well, here's the thing - leadership is a journey, not a destination. It takes time, effort, and practice. But trust me, it's worth it.

Leadership: The Secret Sauce of Success in the Global Market

Folks, let me tell you, leadership is the real deal. It's the difference-maker, the game-changer, the secret sauce that sets the great companies apart from the good ones. And in today's global market, it's more important than ever.

Think about it. The world is getting smaller, and the competition is getting fiercer. Everyone's got access to the same information, the same technology, and the same talent pool. So, what sets the winners apart? Leadership.

A great leader is like a great investor - they've got a vision, they've got a plan, and they've got the guts to see it through. They're not afraid to take calculated risks, to challenge the status quo, and to make tough decisions.

And let me tell you, it pays off. Companies with strong leadership outperform their peers, outlast their competitors, and outdo their expectations.

So, what makes a great leader? It's not about charisma, or charm, or even IQ. It's about integrity, intelligence, and a whole lot of hard work.

It's about setting clear goals, communicating effectively, and empowering your team to achieve greatness.

It's about being adaptable, resilient, and willing to learn from your mistakes. And most importantly, it's about putting your people first - your customers, your employees, and your partners.

So, if you want to succeed in the global market, don't just focus on the numbers, or the products, or the profits. Focus on leadership. Because in the end, that's what will set you apart, and take you to the top. Here's the continuation of the summary in the writing style of Warren Buffet:

Now, I know what you're thinking - "Warren, this all sounds great, but how do I find these leaders?" Well, my friends, it's not easy. But I'll give you a hint - it starts with culture. You see, a great leader can't exist in a vacuum. They need a culture that supports them, empowers them, and inspires them to be their best selves. And that's what I look for when I invest in companies - a culture of leadership.

It's the companies that prioritize their people, their customers, and their values that will outlast the competition. It's the companies that invest in their leaders, that develop them, and that trust them to make the right decisions.

And let me tell you, it's not just about the CEO. Leadership is everywhere - in every department, in every team, and every individual. So, don't just focus on finding the next great CEO.

Focus on building a culture of leadership. Focus on developing the leaders of tomorrow. And most importantly, focus on being a leader yourself. Because in the end, leadership is not just about title or position It's about character, integrity, and a commitment to excellence.

And if you can find that, if you can build that, and if you can live that - then you'll be unstoppable.

"In a world that's moving at the speed of light, your leadership team is the only thing that can keep you ahead of the curve. But you've got to know how to unleash their power.

First, you've got to think differently. Don't just assemble a team of yes-men and women. Find people who are crazy enough to think they can change the world. And then, give them the freedom to do it.

Second, make them own it. Give them a stake in the game. Make them responsible for the success of the company. And then, get out of their way.

Third, stay hungry, stay foolish. Keep pushing the boundaries of what's possible. Keep innovating, keep disrupting, and always, always keep moving forward.

Fourth, merge the dots. Connect the dots between your team members, between departments, and between ideas. Create a culture of collaboration, of innovation, and of experimentation.

And finally, don't be afraid to cannibalize yourself. Don't be afraid to disrupt your business model, your products, and your services. Because if you don't, someone else will.

Your leadership team is your greatest asset. But it's up to you to unlock their potential. So, go ahead, think differently, and change the world."

And remember, innovation is not just about technology. It's about people, it's about culture, and it's about leadership. It's about creating a vision that inspires, that motivates, and that empowers.

Your leadership team should be the catalyst for change, not the barrier. They should be the ones who challenge the status quo, who question the assumptions, and who push the boundaries.

So, don't just build a leadership team, build a movement. Build a movement that inspires, motivates, and that empowers. Build a movement that changes the world.

And always, always remember, the ones who are crazy enough to think they can change the world, are the ones who do.

In a world that's moving at the speed of light, your leadership team is the only thing that can keep you ahead of the curve. So, make them own it, merge the dots, stay hungry, stay foolish, and always, always think differently.

Because in the end, it's not about the technology, it's not about the products, and it's not about the services. It's about the people, it's about the culture, and it's about the leadership. It's about creating a vision tha inspires, that motivates, and that empowers. And that's what will chang the world."

The emergence of AI has significantly impacted the way we create leadership teams that foster innovation. Here are some key ways:

1. Data-driven decision-making: AI provides leaders with data-driven insights, enabling them to make informed decisions and identify areas for innovation.

2. Enhanced talent identification: AI-powered tools help identify top talent with the skills and mindset required for innovative leadership.

3. Personalized development: AI-driven learning platforms offer personalized development opportunities for leaders to enhance their innovation skills.

4. Diverse perspectives: AI can help identify and include diverse perspectives in leadership teams, fostering a culture of innovation.

5. Agile leadership: AI enables leaders to adapt quickly to changing market conditions, fostering an agile and innovative culture.

6. Collaborative leadership: AI facilitates collaboration among leaders, teams, and stakeholders, driving innovation through collective intelligence.

7. Continuous learning: AI supports continuous learning and upskilling for leaders, ensuring they stay ahead of the innovation curve.

8. Innovative problem-solving: AI-powered tools enable leaders to approach problems from new angles, driving innovative solutions.

9. Culture of experimentation: AI encourages a culture of experimentation, allowing leaders to test and refine innovative ideas.

10. Virtual leadership teams: AI enables the creation of virtual leadership teams, bringing together global talent to drive innovation.

By embracing AI, organizations can create leadership teams that drive innovation, stay ahead of the curve, and achieve success in an ever-changing business landscape.

Chapter 9

12 Keys to Fostering Effective Leadership Teams

1. Cultivate a Culture of Trust

   - Principle: Trust is the bedrock of any successful leadership team. When leaders trust each other, decisions are made faster and more effectively. Encourage transparency and integrity in all dealings.

   - Application: Implement open-door policies and regular team-building exercises to build and maintain trust.

2. Hire and Promote the Best Talent

   - Principle: Your leadership team is only as good as the individuals who comprise it. Invest in hiring and promoting top talent who exhibit not only competence but also strong leadership qualities.

- Application: Focus on recruiting top performers and provide them with opportunities for growth and advancement within the organization.

3. Encourage Open Communication

- Principle: Effective communication is crucial for a high-performing leadership team. Encourage open dialogue and the free exchange of ideas to foster innovation and resolve conflicts.

- Application: Hold regular team meetings and encourage feedback from all levels of the organization.

4. Define and Align Vision and Goals

- Principle: A unified vision and clear goals are essential for effective leadership. Ensure that all team members are aligned with the company's vision and understand their roles in achieving it.

- Application: Develop a strategic plan with clear objectives and communicate it effectively throughout the organization.

5. Foster a Culture of Accountability

- Principle: Accountability drives performance. Ensure that each team member understands their responsibilities and the standards to which they are held.

- Application: Establish clear metrics for success and hold regular performance reviews to track progress and address any issues.

6. Empower Decision-Making

- Principle: Effective leaders need autonomy to make decisions. Empower your leadership team by delegating authority and trusting them to act in the best interest of the organization.

- Application: Avoid micromanaging and encourage team members to take initiative and make informed decisions.

7. Invest in Leadership Development

- Principle: Continuous learning is key to effective leadership. Invest in leadership development programs to enhance the skills of your team and prepare them for future challenges.

- Application: Provide training, mentoring, and opportunities for professional development.

8. Promote Collaboration and Teamwork

- Principle: Collaboration enhances problem-solving and drives success. Encourage teamwork and create opportunities for leaders to work together on projects.

- Application: Use collaborative tools and foster a team-oriented environment that values diverse perspectives.

9. Recognize and Reward Excellence

- Principle: Recognition and rewards motivate and retain top talent. Acknowledge achievements and celebrate successes to boost morale and incentivize performance.

- Application: Implement a recognition program and ensure that outstanding contributions are rewarded appropriately.

10. Maintain Flexibility and Adaptability

- Principle: The business landscape is constantly changing. Effective leadership teams must be flexible and adaptable to navigate challenges and seize new opportunities.

- Application: Encourage a mindset of continuous improvement and be open to revising strategies as needed.

11. Focus on Long-Term Value

- Principle: Effective leadership teams focus on creating long-term value rather than short-term gains. Ensure that decisions are made with the long-term success of the organization in mind.

- Application: Align team goals with the company's long-term vision and prioritize sustainable growth.

12. Foster a Positive and Inclusive Culture

- Principle: A positive and inclusive culture enhances team cohesion and productivity. Promote an environment where diversity is valued, and everyone feels included and respected.

- Application: Implement policies that support diversity and inclusion, and actively work to create a positive workplace culture.

Conclusion

Fostering an effective leadership team requires a blend of trust, communication, and strategic focus. By prioritizing these key elements, organizations can reduce attrition rates, enhance performance, and ultimately improve profit margins. Remember, the strength of a company lies in its leadership team, and investing in these areas will yield long-term benefits.

Made in United States
North Haven, CT
24 August 2024

56418290R20029